M

La'Tasha Perez

BookLeaf
Publishing

India | USA | UK

Presentation by *BookLeaf Publishing*

Web: www.bookleafpub.com

E-mail: info@bookleafpub.com

ISBN: 9789358369250

First edition 2023

DEDICATION

To those who live one foot on each side of cultural lines, those who have been hurt by a love you thought you'd never repair, to those who struggle with mental health and deal with waves of grief, I see you. I am you.

Let's heal together.

ACKNOWLEDGEMENT

Thank you to my several muses and to my Crow, I can never thank you enough for your love, gentleness and support in every challenge I've taken on.

Special thank you to my daughter, Kaylah Marie, who has heard every version of every poem, kept me company while I wrote all night and took down the random notes that I was able to snatch from my racing thoughts.

PREFACE

Let's Start at the Beginning, shall we…

I have always enjoyed reading poetry. The flow and rhythm were magical to me. The many mysteries that lay behind the words were something to be unlocked. I always wondered what the author was trying to convey and if we ever truly get it just right. Maybe we miss the mark completely, maybe we put too much of ourselves into the interpretations of the poetry. But then I wonder, isn't that what it is all about, the interpretation. How we, the reader, choose to interpret what is there in print. I know I have read the same poem at different times in my life and each time, it has told me different things because I have looked at it with a new perspective. I started writing poetry around the age of nine years old when I read Edgar Allan Poe's Annabel Lee. I was forever enchanted by the beauty of the language in which he used to declare his love for his darling Annabel Lee. It was then that I realized that I loved words. Being clever enough to string words together in a way to convey feelings and emotions to others was a skill I wanted. I wanted nothing more than to be able to influence others with my writing.

So, I set off to the library every day, pouring over poetry books at every chance I got. I started my hand at simple subjects, love for my family, my cat, my friends, and my dreams. They were horrible. I was self-taught. I didn't know what a simile was or even a metaphor. I had no idea what I was doing. So, I gave up the idea that I would ever become a poet and began writing children's stories.

When I got into high school, I gave up children's stories and began writing creative nonfiction. I didn't know that is what it was called at the time, I was just writing little moments in time about my life that I found to be important to me. Then in college, I took a creative writing class where we would produce a book at the end. With more knowledge than I ever imagined I could absorb from this wonderful poet, I was lucky to have as a teacher, I decided to try my hand at writing poetry again. I focused more on my creative nonfiction work but still worked on my poetry. Not convinced I would ever call myself a poet, though. I produced a few poems I can honestly say I was proud of; however, they were not accepted into the book. Two of my fiction pieces were and 3 of my creative nonfiction pieces were.

Now in college and with a better sense of who I was, I set off on a journey to find what drives me so I had a better idea of what I wanted to write about. I grew up sheltered in a mostly Mexican household and my Dine (Navajo) side was never really discussed too often. Neither was my Spaniard side. So, I started to research on my own and found so many injustices that tore at my heartstrings. I started reading Langston Hughes, Phillis Wheatley, and Allen Ginsberg, to name a few. I realized poetry didn't have to be hearts and flowers. It could be hard, difficult and in your face. And that was the kind of poet I wanted to be. I wanted others to hear through word and emotion the turmoil, fears and oppression of my people, gender and even myself. But I still had no idea how to do this or where to start. Because If I'm being truthful, I was afraid. I was afraid of people knowing my secrets and who I was.

I started with less traumatizing poems, mostly about the strength of my children and the Diné blood that runs through their veins from their ancestors and the love and nurturing of my brothers. I soon found myself wandering into darker, scarier subjects like mental health with the help of reading Optimism One, violence against women and children, and drug and alcohol abuse. I kept these safely hidden and showed no one. They were raw and angry. I was angry. They seemed unfinished, unpolished and

I was not ready for the world to see how angry I was at it for the wrongdoings of others. I needed more training and lessons, I needed to read more. I took another creative writing class and learned even more. I started branching out of my comfort zone and writing more metaphorically, which I found suited my writing style in poetry as well as creative nonfiction. I was in a calmer place mentally and prepared to once again pick up the pen and pour out my soul on paper.

This collection of poems is mixed with heartbreak, death, injustices, mental health, rebellion and a dreamer's imagination. My hope in pouring myself into these words is that it will bring you comfort. Comfort in knowing you are not alone, maybe a call to action, imagination to the greatest extent, and value of your worth.

My Scars and All

Born to a strong-willed stubborn
seventeen-year-old girl, I was raised in a world
sheltered by love, but it could not prepare me for
all that I've had to endure. The streets and drugs
called to her like a siren calls to men at sea.
After losing me, her love was stronger than
before and she came back to claim what was
rightfully hers. She met my step-dad and bore 3
boys. Those boys were my life. My everything. I
watched them grow and nurtured them as if they
were my own. I was the sunflower in the garden
watching over them, patiently waiting for them
to grow and flourish into young men. But I knew
the streets would soon come for them too. I
fiercely protected them. Kept them from drugs
and alcohol. Kept their heads in books and feet
on skateboards. Then I met a boy when I was
seventeen. And my boys drifted down a path I
could not follow. I didn't like this boy, but he
was persistent. With that much devotion and
adoration, how could I not give him a chance. I
was soon intoxicated with his charms. And in
two years' time, I was living with him. That's
when the cheating started. That's when the
manipulation and manhandling started. That's

when self-loathing and suicidal thoughts started
to consume me. And soon angry scars littered
my body. Rescued by my mom and Tia, I was
whisked away. Never to see him again.
Sometime later I met another man, and bore him
3 children. Married life seemed to suit me. I
worked, went to college, cared for my babies
and husband and my household. Married life
however did not suit him. He was overwhelmed
and overworked. The pressures got to him and
he became a raging alcoholic. Blamed for every
wrong in our marriage. Blamed for the
miscarriage of our twins. I found myself filing
for divorce. Now free, I am finishing my college
degree. Showing my children that obstacles are
just that, obstacles to be overcome. I am now in
my happy place. Writing freely, loving openly,
and cherishing moments with loved ones.

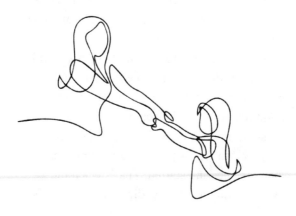

Yá'át'ééh, shidine'é LaTasha Perez, yinishyé The Heart of the Tribe

The spiritual world is nothing new to me,
I know that every day as long as I stay true
Great spirit hears all my prayers and pleas
And will always get me through

The twisting turns the uphill battles
Did I make the right choice at that turn back
there?
Instead of California maybe I belong in Seattle?
Maybe back to Arizona where we ain't rare.

To be close to my kin, even though I ain't in
And to the places I pray would accept me,
but I don't know my clan, so it must be a sin
I feel as if they will only reject me

I don't speak the language, I don't have all the
right features
But I give offerings daily, go to ceremonies and
smudge
Fuck quantum, my heart is "Other", a "savage
creature"

And, no, you can't tell me shit, cuz I will never
budge.

On my beliefs, my desires, destination or my
dreams
I know where life is taking me, I see it now, so
fuckin clearly
The blinding vision sent from my ancestors
glows and gleams
Creator, please remove from my life those that
been insincerely

cuz who is my emergency contact
Loving me, caring for me, saying they'd be there
for me
Alone though, I open up myself to spiritual
attack
It's always been just me, but that's how I stay
free

So, knock me down, its ok, I just get back up
And, that's just proof of the anointing on my life
Cuz, you know we weren't born with a silver
spoon or a golden cup.
And I hear you Shimá, I'll make you proud in
the afterlife.

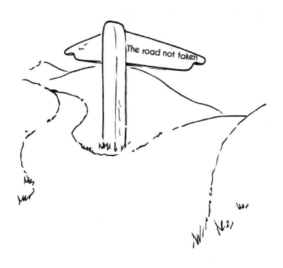

The road not taken

Dear Suicide

You foreign predator, you evil parasite,
How dare you try to destroy my own self.
Depression is no joke; I know all too well.
Deep angry scars mar my brown skin.

Late at night I dream of a semi-perfect world,
Of the moon and the lost boys and pixie dust,
Of flying high past Orion's Belt,
Beyond the galaxy unknown.

In the afternoon I pray that someday
A prince will sweep me off my feet and slay
The demons deep inside my head that lurk and
The ones that say that I am unworthy.

In the morning I wake to a cold sun.
She does nothing to warm this iced bitter heart.
How do I make you understand?
You have no business here, my foe.

Oh, Suicide!
You are still nothing more to me.
Weak as I am, I am much stronger than you.
I am braver and tougher than you may think.
You may not have my life,

                    Signed,
                          Me.

Inescapable Fear

Shoulders rising, chest heaving, tears streaming, my body is heavy.
Like quicksand? Nah. like the secrets from my past haunting my dreams.
Contorted face gasping for breath, yet, lungs screaming, my body is on fire.
Like all the rage within me is an inferno mixed with my desires. burning me alive.
Sweaty palms, a tingling in my hands that race up my arms. My body yearns for freedom.
Like millions of bees swarming just under the surface of my skin, begging to be set free.
Dizziness spreads throughout my brain, making my body go limp. My body will soon give out.
Like a prized fighter, Life has not knocked me down quite yet. I will survive this round.
It consumes me from the inside out and chokes me from within. My body will not survive.
Like a terrified animal, I crouch and hide and wait for it to end, but it goes on forever. It never ends.
Then all of a sudden it is gone and I am free. I can breathe again; I live to tell another tale.

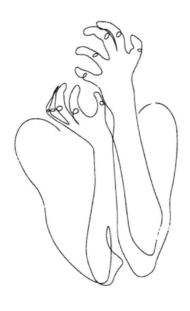

Rage

His friend was his backbone, his friend was his
aid,
His friend was right beside him whenever he
became enraged.
I couldn't change his friend no matter how much
I tried,
I couldn't change his friend for he tore me up
inside.
He would hit me really hard till my eyes were
black and blue,
My boyfriend wouldn't stop him, there was
nothing I could do.
He'd tell me that he hates me, he'd say he didn't
care, I didn't want him around me,
But I didn't tell him, I didn't dare.
He hurt me oh so bad, you really wouldn't
believe, but I was never strong enough,
Never strong enough to leave.
So, I sit here slowly dying, being mentally
abused, God I wish I wasn't crying,
Because he seems very amused.
Now he knows he got me, got me where it hurts,
I must try to end it,
I must end this cursed curse.

He's been so mean to me, and never stopped to think that I
would take my life in an instant,
I would do it in a blink.
One day his friend will hurt him, one day he will betray him.
You see, his friendship is so expensive,
That it is with my life he will repay him.

Forever Stains

I'm that savage beast they warned you about
Plus, I got that Chicana fire.
Come to seek revenge, be successful to all ends
Because, Navajo Pride is something to admire

Through storytelling and picking up that pen
I walk the walk and talk the talk,
Ready to teach all about Sand Creek,
About the Trail of Tears and The Long Walk.

Go ahead, tear down monuments and erase your
ugly past,
Like the eternal sunshine of your spotless sin.
But my children's blood will lament the pain,
And the white of their skin will get them in.

Get them into places I will never be allowed,
Too brown for you, wrong language for us,
The sins of a medicine man
And a Spaniard woman falling in love

Three generations later here I am,
Ball of Confusion, made up of barbed wire,
Wrapped in pretty brown lace.
Apologies if I seem blunt, I'm tired

And you don't know the shit I've been through,
So, for every hurt you inflict upon me
I inflict upon myself like forever stains
But I will always be me, unapologetically.

Wall of Thorns

Guarded. Well beyond thick, sharp, prickly
thorns
Is a fragile thing. Never to be spoken of again.
Well forgotten and never to be loved again.
Never to be touched or caressed ever again.
Time will harden her. Her beat will slow.
She will darken, shrivel away.
Locked away for all eternity.
Don't look, don't you dare.
For if you do, I swear,
She will be no more,
She will splinter,
She will break.
Leave her be.
I pray
thee.

Unconquerable

They came unto my land
My ears flatten and my gray-speckled fur stands
on end
My heavy paws pound on the thick white snow,
As I race back to my tribe, to my pack.
My breath comes out in white puffs of smoke
I skid to a stop. Nearly tripping over paws too
big.
I let out a mighty howl.
Will my brothers and sisters hear me?
Will my warriors come in time?
Will we protect our elders and our young?
I howl again.
My brothers and sisters will come.
I take off once more, like the bear ready to
defend.
Tearing through the tall trees,
Splashing across the ice-cold streams,
My ears perk as I hear the ferocious howls of my
family.
They have come to destroy and conquer us.
We are indigenous to these lands.
My brothers and sisters will come.
My snout too big for my head, as I am still
growing, sniffs the air.

I smell them near, but
They will not take our land from us.
My brothers and sisters will come.
My once smooth fur catches on branches as I
tear through the brush.
Ripping fur and skin from my body, but I don't
feel a thing
The adrenaline races through my veins with the
blood of my ancestors
Urging me to push through the pain and carry
on.
Because we are here to stay.

And my brothers and sisters WILL come.

Slave mentality

Education as a nation is a foundation,
Coalition arbitration, castration,
Carnation, inhalation, elation
Filtration, fixation, temptation.
Ejaculation, ovulation, gestation.
Inflation, liberation, freedom nation.

Chains lead to sprains and pains
Bloodstains remains hurricanes
Campaigns detains membranes
Warplanes gains plains
Domains complain about reigns
Abstains outgains and detains

Dead said, "go ahead"
Watershed chrome red, crowned head
Mislead unfed frybread
Spearhead, unwed warhead
Dragon's head, feather bed, seeing red
Bloodshed, thrust ahead, hospital bed.

Mestizo Crown

The domineering Spaniard that sits on my left
shoulder wants to sit on the other as well.
The proud Navajo that sits on my right
tells that damn Spaniard, "To you I will NEVER
sell."
My hard working Mexican is too busy to care.
Yet, she's right here within the very being of my
soul, telling them to share.

Do you see the blue tint of the blood in my
veins?
The conquistador itching to invade through my
skin.
Do you see the savage beast discipline, then
cuddle her young?
My war face beautifully painted with colored
mud.

You see light brown skin, hazel eyes, dark
brown hair.
I say Mixed. But your census says white. So, I'll
say other, But, you don't even care.
The lion roar that rips through my lips
Has protected me more than it has neglected me

So, for every name that you hurl at me, I'll
devour and spit back out.
Not an American. Not, dare I say a Human.
Just look down. Your shadow looks like mine,
therefore, you are my kin.
Yet, I feel like the alien; in my own skin. Like no
side will ever win, this race war within.
You look at me and see a lighter shade of brown
But, fuck you, while I straighten my Mestizo
crown.

Weakness

As the tears threaten to consume me
My eyes struggle against the foreign invaders.
Like the Grand Canyon, my eyes know not what
to do, but to reject and refuse
to allow the alien wetness to slip through and
parade weakness down my face
like some poor pitiful fool.
I do not allow it.
Within my depths I am flooded, but you will
never see me break.
Too Proud.
Too Stubborn.
Too Foolish.
Maybe this is my weakness
not my strength.

Love Language for a Rose

When people ask you what is your love
language; physical touch, quality time, words of
affirmation, acts of service or receiving gifts.
These are the 5 we think of.
But what about MUSIC… I believe my mom's
was music. And I think I got that from her…

Music was always played in my home growing
up… I ALWAYS knew what kind of mood the
day was leaning towards based on the music that
drifted down the hallway to my room, softly
nudging me awake.

Was it Faith Hill's "It matters to me," or Lorrie
Morgan's "What part of No?" Would I come out
to see her standing at the already squeaky clean
sliding glass door? Staring at something I could
not see. Some past hurt I could not understand.
A hurt she would spend my entire teenage years
trying to shield me from by keeping me
forbidden to do literally anything, especially
date.
Would I wake up to Grupo Límite's "Solo
Contigo?" I would army crawl down the hallway
and peek from behind the couch to watch her

sweeping our tiny kitchen swaying her hips, moving her hands and arms in perfect rhythm to the beat. The accordion was one of my favorite sounds. She was so beautiful. I couldn't wait to grow up and be just like her. Her box-dyed super straight Indian hair had volume! How?! How did it have volume? I loved her more than anything.

Would it be Debbie Debb's "Lookout Weekend?" I'd dance my way down the hallway doing my fancy footwork she taught me like a boss as she'd meet me halfway smiling and laughing. Her laugh was infectious. Loud. Boisterous. Obnoxious. You couldn't help but laugh with her. We would stare at each other challenging the other with more and more fierce moves until she would start to vogue, making me crack up and lose concentration. She was never fair. She said life wasn't.

Would it be Los Tucanes de Tijuana's "El Tucanazo?"
I'd run to the living room waiting eagerly for my turn to be tossed around like a rag doll. She never ran out of breath. Me and Joshy would be dying on the floor giggling and she would still be hopping around one foot to the other, in perfect synchronization to the music perfectly

swinging in to the next song, usually "La Chona."

Or maybe it was gonna be The Whispers' "Rock Steady?"
We knew we were about to get down. She was gonna bring out all the moves. She would sit all 4 of us on the couch, Me, Joshy, Elijah and Anthony and sing to us. We would clap to the beat, cheer her on, then she'd bring us down, hold my hand as I held the boys and we'd all dance together as she held onto newborn baby Anthony on her swinging hip.

Maybe Smokey Norful's "I need you now" or Nicole C. Mullen's "My Redeemer Lives" I would go get on my knees next to her, put my little hand on her back as she was bowed down sobbing into the floor. I'd lift my other hand and cry out silently to a God she so desperately believed could take her pain away. But every time I saw her like this, I questioned why he didn't or worse, wouldn't. She would say she was lost. And that in life I would often get lost. But that it's in the finding myself again that would matter. She would say we didn't need 4 walls and people gossiping to praise God. That we could do it anywhere. Of course in a church, but also in our home, in the car, in the grocery store. As long as I believed he died for my sins and I lived my life trying not to sin and continued bringing lost souls to him then I would be ok. She believed it was her duty to save the broken and lost because she was broken and lost too.

But mostly we woke up to the likes of "Angel Baby," "I'm your Puppet," "Tell it like it is," "Baby you got it." We knew we were going to clean up so we could have a last-minute kickback and invite people over. She loved to host. She Loved to feed people. Not just their bellies but their souls. She'd give her last smile she could muster just so they could too. Her last laugh, the only hug she could give because she was breaking inside herself. She said whenever someone hugged you always let them let go first, you never know how long they will need your comfort. Even though she was physically born with a hole in her heart, her heart was whole and purer than anyone I have ever known. She loved having a houseful. Didn't matter that we weren't celebrating anything. Just the fact that we were all there. Together. Listening to music.

I see a lot of myself in my mom. I hated hearing people tell me I looked exactly like her or that I reminded them of her. She would always sing to

me "she get it from her momma" But, oh, What
I would give to hear her sing it to me just once
more.

I wish I could hand you the AUX right now
mom. I wonder what you would play today?

A Cousin's love

Our hair is blowing in the hot valley wind,
I look up to my big sister, watch her- you see my
profile.
She spreads her arms wide. Like an eagle- free.
You see her back.
Her left hand holding my big cousin Corinna's
right hand
While I hold Corinna's left.
Corinna's vivid red hair ruffles wild with the
breeze.
A vast golden field lay ahead of us.
The perfect, cloudless blue sky meets the
horizon,
Dots of lush green trees sprinkle the crease of
that horizon.
The lake jutting forward, curving like a serpent,
And disappearing. Clever like that serpent.
The quiet here is peaceful.
The Love here is strong.
The bond is unfailing.

In Loving Memory of Corinna 1998-2015

Moonlight

How many times have you gone with me to
chase the moon?
I've already lost count, but I know it's coming to
an end, all too soon.
Wasting gas but never time, cuz the world falls
away
and time doesn't even exist when I'm with you.
Our lips find one another in the black void, slow
longing kisses under the stars,
Our only witness out here is passing trains and
passing cars
Crickets chirp incessantly, while the frogs also
make themselves known and a howl from an
animal we listen for in the dark and unknown.
My car lookin so sleek in the moonlight but I
only have eyes for you.
Wrapped in your arms, safe and warm, I just
want to make all your dreams come true.
We share secrets not another soul on earth will
ever know. I take that shit to the grave
Cus the love we share took time to grow, damn,
I think I'll always be love's slave

How many times have my gasps startled you,
thinkin we were in trouble?

Only to roll your eyes at my childlike squeal cuz
I saw a stray, I know I'm never subtle.
The way you embrace my every flaw and tell me
sweet things, The way you make me see me for
me, the way you kiss away all my hurt and make
my heart sing.
Talkin about singin, shoot you know I love
music. We be bumpin them oldies daily talking
bout "I like the way you love me," "Baby, I'm
for real," and "LaLa Means I Love You."
The way my body instantly relaxes when I'm
with you, cuz I know I'm safe with you, I know
I can tell you anything and you won't say a
word. And vice versa cuz you know I got you,
that's just how we do.

How many times under the blanket of the night
sky, with no other soul around but you and I,
Have we spoken of our dreams, our hopes and
our fears, often leaving you to kiss away my
falling tears
Pulling me close in the crisp cool air, something
inside me begins to stir,
The Crow's dark eyes watch me as I begin to
purr.
Igniting the fire within, and trying not to sin.
You were my answered prayers, sent to me in
my time of need, and as crazy as I can be you
have never even raised your voice at me.

Rumors began to spread, but it didn't even phase us, cuz we just let that shit go dead.
Then people wonder why we keep things quiet.
Shit, sometimes I just be wanting to riot.

How many times have I walked away because we want different things?
Love is not all you need. And, honestly, being the same person kinda stings.
I'm not a part of your world, and you won't let me be,
So, for now let's chase the moon, and maybe one day, you'll set me free.

A Dreamer's Wish List

Soft butterfly kisses on the chest of my lover
Periwinkle pixie dust sprinkled on my head just
to flutter
Through the open window out to the night sky
Blue as the ocean, I spread my arms and fly
The cool mist touches my skin, the moisture is
papery thin
It's wet and it's frigid cold, it's delightful as sin.
The tip of the cloud touches my toes
As feathers of jaybirds tickle my nose
I glance at the scene way down below
A city of light befallen with snow
The sweet caress as it melts on my skin

Wish I had 3 wishes from a lamp of a djin
I'd rub that pretty bottle so smooth and so bright
Till the world fell away and all was just right
Diamond encrusted sparkling with gold
Rubies so red what a beauty to behold
The lamp itself is a treasure all on its own
And the djinn inside is forever alone
I know his pain but don't give him pity,

For he is a mischievous one, evil and gritty
I wish I had a guardian angel to watch as I fall

For every time I'm on the ground, I stall for a
divine call
Hair golden blonde, wings blinding white
if you stare too long, you may forever lose sight
His aesthetic is so perfect and so very pure
Adonis would be jealous, I am almost sure

But I do not have these things, I am only me,
Skin, bone, flesh and blood. The only thing I can
be.
I slowly come back to earth, back to reality.
And realize that, nothing holds me back but me
and gravity.
The comfort of my warm sweet bed, and of my
lover's strong arms
Keep me safe until I dream again of pixie dust
and other charms.

Show me your Garden

Show me your cobblestone pathway. The one sprinkled with moss, worn, cracked and stained leading to the depths of your garden locked and hidden away.

Show me your swinging gate with the intricately designed brass key, harboring peaceful nights and sunny days.

Show me your silly gnomes. Let me explore and fall in love with each one.

Show me fuzzy caterpillars and the creepy crawlers who find harmony within your florals by your enchanting roses, blood red, perfect and full of thorns.

Show me your Sunflowers, bold, bright, face warmed by the sun's soft kisses and the small patch of enticing lavender, swaying in the light breeze, letting off its pleasant aromatic scent.

Show me your weeping willow tree. An elegant force to be reckoned with, yet vulnerable where

safety and comfort are hidden within their
graceful embrace

Show me your dying fauna you have yet to heal.
Fading, bent and bruised petals and leaves
waiting for a tender touch.

Show me your roots. Dirty, brown, tangled deep
within the soil, intertwining with Mother Earth.

Show me the dirt patch, all the way in the back,
the spot patiently waiting for something special
to belong within it.

And in that place we shall see if your garden has
a place for me.

Flame

Look, I know I'm difficult and I always got
some shit to say
But it's cuz I see you, the real you, the one that
others tend to push aside, or even push away.
I know you see him too; your eyes starting to
open to his beauty within,
He seems far away right now I know, but keep
going, life is about the journey, not the win.

I'll be your friend for always and forever, you do
whatever you want to,
I won't stop you,
I'll support your dreams, I'll support all your
hustles,
you can even talk to me about the girls who ain't
true.
I may talk a lil shit cuz boy you grown, you
knew them girls ain't with it, they were just
somethin to do.
They don't see you for you, but like I said, do
you boo. You just ain't ready for me. I'm only
your friend until you realize who you truly want
to be.

See, I'm not for house play, I was made to be a wife. An equal counterpart. To be placed at your side, to cherish and protect.
Homie, I'll be the greatest love of your life.
And from within that space you provide, in the protective bubble by your side, comes a real love that will never stray, never put you in a position where you feel you need to hide.
And I will trust you to take us where we need to be, so hand me your ego, as I lay down my pride.

Yes, I'm independent as fuck, but only because I need to be.
But, I want to navigate this world with you to help you become all that you can be.
My inquisitive mind will throw random questions at you on the daily like a detective.
But keep in mind I'm just curious, I mean, ok yea maybe a lil protective
Of my heart, my soul, my peace, but ok boo, you do what you gotta do,
cuz, Creator knows I had that era too.

And when you're tired of the silly games, and ready to settle down and see me, I pray that I can still be that for you.
Still be your one true friend, the one you been wanting, the one who let you do you,

Unfortunately, I got a feeling that maybe I'll be
tucked away in someone else's side.
Someone that saw me, the real me, you know,
the one you pushed aside

Offering

A pinch of tobacco I borrowed with all the intent
of repaying
And with it I also offer up my broken heart
while praying
For a miraculous and undeserved healing
For the healers to find whatever my body is
concealing
My broken womb cries from within,
A burning sensation, delicious as sin
The warmth spreads into my belly, into my legs,
into my chest
I feel her love, her intense caress, I pray she
chose me to bless

The disconnected tissue deep down begins to
repair and discover
A whole new side of life I was meant to recall
and recover
And then her face appears in the most
unexpected place
Lovin on me from the surface of my vase
I take in her love and grace as she smiles upon
my face
A longing from within I don't want to ever
replace

The intense feeling of love, comfort and desire
Let me choose the right divine that will give me
all that I require
To bring birth to everything life has to gift me in
this universe
I'll use my gifts wisely to navigate life and break
this generational curse.

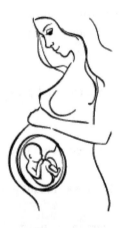

You

"what's me?" he whispers
Does she feel it too deep within her
For the rest of my life, I just want to make her
stir
Make her purr, make her smile, Have fun with
her inner child
I don't know what it is about her, but I like that
she's kinda wild
I see she been through some shit and I just
wanna protect her
Reassure her and never neglect her.
Does she see a King? Or a knight with a
weakness in his armor?
But I am not weak, that sacrifice makes me
strong in my honor.

"You don't feel it?"
I fell asleep in your arms
And was disarmed by your charms
I don't think you realize just who you are?
You are my king, my one true star.
The one that was sent from the Creator above
My one and only, my Greatest Love.

The one that will permanently transform our lives
Never wanted to remarry, but I will forever be your wife.
I will lay down my life, my ego, my pride,
If you down for me, forever I'll ride.
I got your back, through it all,
I'll even catch you, when you fall.

"....."
I don't know what she means?
Does she know she's my Queen?
How do I tell her I'm not ready for this?
How do I turn away from this bliss?
I never want her to leave me or go
I wanna take my time with her and do this thing slow

"Do you want me to leave?"
Oh no that's how I know.
His presence is so pure, addicting as snow
I want to stay here with my head on his shoulder
He anticipates my needs, He's for sure my beholder
Of my desires and my dreams
I'm falling apart, right at the seams

"...."
She knows, I see it, in her gentle aura

And soon a seed will plant, we'll just call her
Isadora
In time our love will expand beyond reason
If loving her is wrong, then charge me with
treason
She's lookin up at me with those bright eyes
So gentle, so strong, so loving and wise
She's waiting for me to give her an answer,
But am I ready for this, am I ready to romance
her?

Imagination Island

There's this place inside my head, I often
disappear to.
I know it's my future cuz man if you only knew,
The intense feelings, the surrealness of this
random phenomenon,
I see it there, I'm The Queen, raised from a
pawn.
I'm finally safe here and no one can ever again
say to me,
"You wouldn't have that without me, you
wouldn't have that if it wasn't for me."

I'm just me abundantly and I will only ever see
the beauty
And wonder within my dreams and I will always
do my duty
To me, my children, my tribe even as I struggle
with my healing,
Sometimes I'm hard-headed, and that's just so
revealing
But on the Island, I escape almost daily
As I listen to the sounds of my daughter's
Ukelele
Drifting from the sandy shores below,

I flow to the sweet melody hand in hand with
my crow

A modest cottage, surrounded with ferns, herbs
and fauna
A whole field of lavender, roses, sunflowers and
marijuana
Lush green high hills, and deep valley depths
A beautiful place as this, aint no problem getting
my 10k steps
Every bird of every color raises up and takes
flight
I join them as they encircle me and I know I'll
always be alright
So, I'll just take a nap in my garden and stare up
at the stars
While I wait for you in this place I call ours.

Printed in the USA
CPSIA information can be obtained
at www.ICGtesting.com
CBHW020958120824
12967CB00039B/1503

9 789358 369250